THE GREAT ART ACTIVITY BOOK

Paul thurlby

Hodder
Children's
Books

It's raining in Paris!
Decorate the umbrellas.

THE UMBRELLAS, about 1881–6
PIERRE-AUGUSTE RENOIR

Pierre-Auguste Renoir began this picture in 1881, but it was left unfinished. When he went back to it a few years later, he had developed a much crisper painting style. That is why the lady on the left looks sharper than the little girl holding the hoop on the right.

Can you put these paintings in the order they were painted? Label 1 as the oldest and 4 as the most recent.

ANSWERS

THE WILTON DIPTYCH, about 1395–9
Unknown – English or French

THE AMBASSADORS, 1533
Hans Holbein the Younger

BALLET DANCERS, about 1890–1900
Hilaire-Germain-Edgar Degas

GET IT ON, 2016
Paul Thurlby

What is in this mirror's reflection?
Use your pencils to decide.

THE ARNOLFINI PORTRAIT, 1434
Jan van Eyck

This portrait is as puzzling as it is famous. Who are the man and woman, and what sort of ceremony is taking place? Two shadowy figures are reflected in the mirror on the wall. The inscription above it reads, 'Jan van Eyck was here 1434'.

It's time to spot the stripes. Can you find each of these details in the jungle scene?

ANSWERS

SURPRISEDI, 1891
HENRI ROUSSEAU

You can almost feel the tropical winds blowing through the grass in Henri Rousseau's painting. This exotic scene is very detailed, but it is a fantasy. Henri had never visited the jungle – his entire life was spent in his homeland of France.

Who, or what, has the knight
speared with his lance?

SAINT GEORGE AND THE DRAGON, about 1470
PAOLO UCCELLO

This painting is about the legend of Saint George. Paolo Uccello has cleverly used the picture to tell two parts of the same tale. On the right, George is shown attacking a dragon. On the left, a princess holds the creature on a chain as if it has already been captured.

Copy this princess into the blank grid, one square at a time.

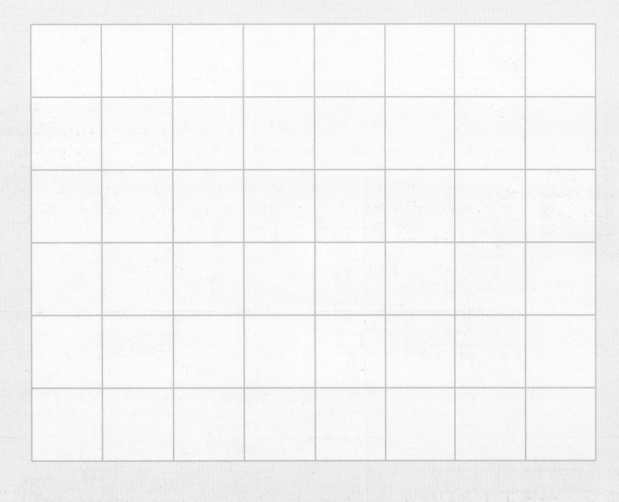

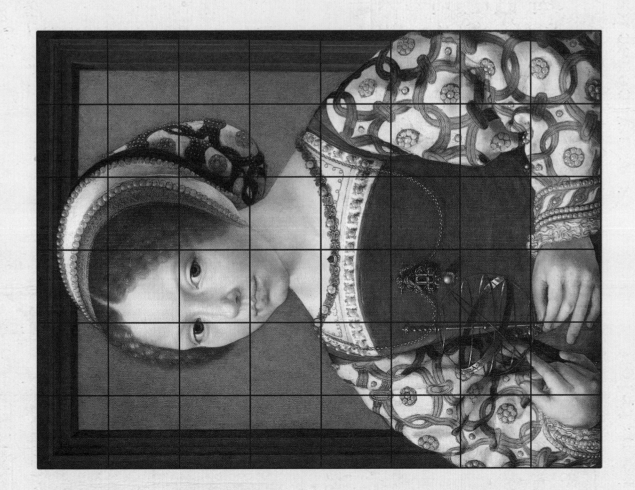

A YOUNG PRINCESS (DOROTHEA OF DENMARK?),
about 1530–2
JAN GOSSAERT

The young lady in this portrait is wearing a beautiful dress and matching headpiece, both of which have been inlaid with hundreds of pearls. Jan Gossaert cleverly painted her in front of a picture frame so that it looks as if she is real.

One of these paintings is not an impressionist painting. Which is it?

ANSWER

THE CONCERT, about 1626
HENDRICK TER BRUGGHEN

The Concert is the odd one out. It was painted over 200 years before the Impressionists. Impressionist painters tended to paint very quickly, trying to capture the movement of light. They often painted outdoors.

This circus star is hanging from the ceiling by her teeth!
Draw in the rest of the astounded audience.

**MISS LA LA AT THE
CIRQUE FERNANDO, 1879**
HILAIRE-GERMAIN-EDGAR DEGAS

Miss La La was a daring trapeze artist – Degas went to sketch her several times when she performed in Paris. He skilfully angled his portrait so that we have to look upwards at Miss La La, making it feel as if we are in the audience, too.

How many of these objects can you spot in this painting?

 ☐ ☐  ☐ ☐ ☐ ☐

ANSWERS

THE ANNUNCIATION, WITH SAINT EMIDIUS, 1486
CARLO CRIVELLI

This work of art was painted over 500 years ago. Carlo Crivelli carefully worked out what the scene would look like if you were standing at the end of this street. His perspective is so accurate, the picture almost looks real.

Draw the other half of Monet's famous bridge.

THE WATER-LILY POND, 1899
Claude Monet

This beautiful scene from Claude Monet's water garden in Giverny, France, is known and loved all over the world. Monet painted the bridge at different times of day and at different times of year, trying to capture the play of light and colours.

This painting features lots of different types of brushstrokes. Finish the scene using dabs of colour to bring it to life.

BATHERS AT ASNIÈRES, 1884
GEORGES SEURAT

Georges Seurat decided to do things a bit differently when he created this hazy scene. He mixed broad brushstrokes with dots of contrasting colour to make the sun appear to shimmer on the water. This use of dots later became known as pointillism.

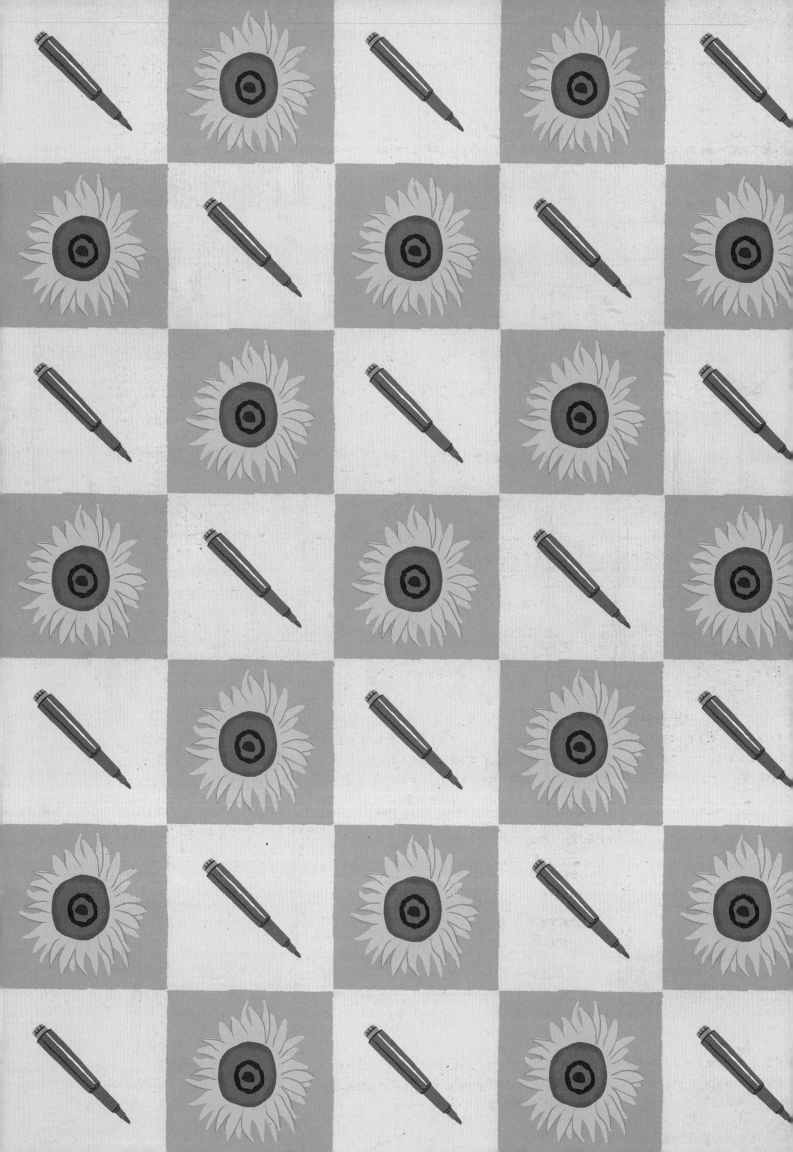

HODDER CHILDREN'S BOOKS

First published in Great Britain in 2018 by Hodder and Stoughton

Illustrations copyright © Paul Thurlby, 2018

Text by Mandy Archer 2018

A CIP record for this book is available from the British Library.

ISBN: 978 1 444 93427 4

10 9 8 7 6 5 4 3 2 1

Printed and bound in China

MIX
Paper from responsible sources
FSC® C104740
FSC www.fsc.org

Hodder Children's Books
An imprint of Hachette Children's Group
Part of Hodder and Stoughton
Carmelite House
50 Victoria Embankment
London
EC4Y 0DZ

An Hachette UK Company
www.hachette.co.uk
www.hachettechildrens.co.uk

MADAME MOITESSIER, 1856
Jean-Auguste-Dominique Ingres

When Ingres first met Madame Moitessier, he was struck by her beauty. He spent so long working on her portrait, her clothing began to look dated. The artist had to re-paint her outfit several times to keep up with the latest fashions.

This artist painted Venice many times throughout his life. Circle the matching pair on the page.

ANSWERS

A REGATTA ON THE GRAND CANAL, about 1740
CANALETTO

VENICE: THE BASIN OF SAN MARCO ON ASCENSION DAY, about 1740
CANALETTO

VENICE: ENTRANCE TO THE CANNAREGIO, probably 1734–42
CANALETTO

VENICE: THE UPPER REACHES OF THE GRAND CANAL WITH S. SIMEONE PICCOLO, about 1740 CANALETTO

A REGATTA ON THE GRAND CANAL, about 1740
CANALETTO

VENICE: S. PIETRO IN CASTELLO, 1730s
CANALETTO

Canaletto painted many landscapes of Venice in Italy. He often painted the Grand Canal. Here he has shown people enjoying the regatta – an annual carnival that still takes place today.

Use the grids to help you sketch your own horse portrait.

WHISTLEJACKET, about 1762
GEORGE STUBBS

This magnificent stallion was called Whistlejacket. In order to show how impressive the creature was, George Stubbs decided to paint it at lifesize. The racehorse is shown rearing up on two legs, with a wild look in its eye.

Study the vases of sunflowers. Which is the odd one out?

SUNFLOWERS, 1888
VINCENT VAN GOGH

This painting is called a still life. It focuses on a vase of sunflowers. Although the subject is very simple, Vincent van Gogh fills the picture with feeling and emotion. The golds and yellows are used to represent friendship, happiness and hope.

Peer into this courtyard. Who might be standing in the doorway? Find a pencil and sketch your idea.

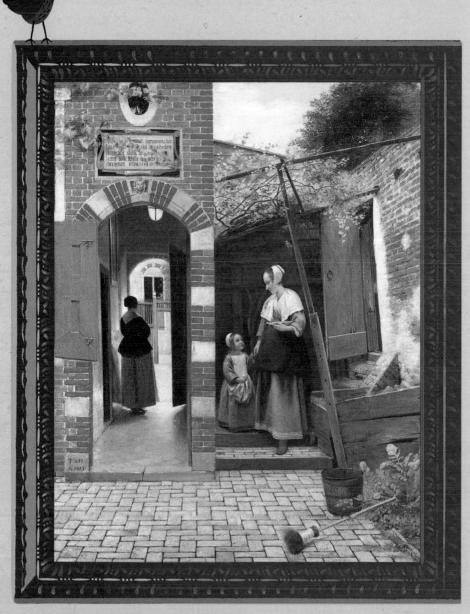

THE COURTYARD OF A HOUSE IN DELFT, 1658
PIETER DE HOOCH

This portrait is packed with detail – every brick, blossom and plank of wood is as perfect as a photograph. We can see a servant in the courtyard holding hands with a small girl. Her mistress is standing in the passageway, looking out to the street.

Fill the frames with self portraits. What did you look like at five years old? Imagine what you might look like in ten or twenty years' time.

SELF PORTRAIT AT THE AGE OF 34, 1640
REMBRANDT

SELF PORTRAIT AT THE AGE OF 63, 1669
REMBRANDT

Rembrandt painted more self portraits than any other artist of the 17th century. In the first picture, Rembrandt presents himself as a confident and successful artist. In the second, nearly 30 years have passed. Now he is an old man, gazing wistfully out from the canvas.

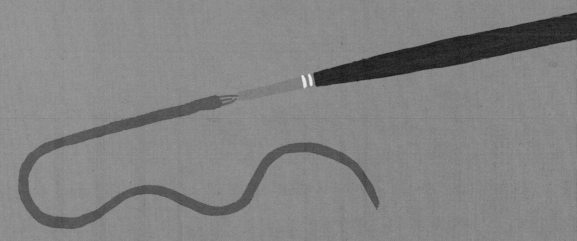

Draw the head and body of Miss Clara, the rhinoceros by Pietro Longhi.

EXHIBITION OF A RHINOCEROS AT VENICE, probably 1751
PIETRO LONGHI

Not many people living in Europe during Pietro Longhi's lifetime would have seen a rhino before. His painting shows a real animal called Miss Clara, put on display at the Venice Carnival. Huge crowds gathered to see such a strange and unusual creature.

What is this lady
watching at the
theatre? Sketch the
rest of the scene.

AT THE THEATRE (LA PREMIÈRE SORTIE) 1876–7
PIERRE-AUGUSTE RENOIR

This young woman is leaning forward in her box seat, keen to see the show. When experts studied Pierre-Auguste's painting, they discovered something interesting. X-rays showed that the artist originally featured two more people in front of the girl.

THE MANCHESTER MADONNA, about 1497
MICHELANGELO

Michelangelo wasn't just a painter, he was a sculptor and an architect, too. This unfinished picture shows us how he used to work. The artist started by painting on a layer of green as an undercoat for the skin, then built up colours on top.

Continue the pattern
of swirling clouds
across the page.

A WHEATFIELD, WITH CYPRESSES, 1889
Vincent van Gogh

This windy wheatfield is full of whirling, swirling brushstrokes! Only the cypress trees stand still and firm against the churning sky. Vincent van Gogh uses this stormy, restless scene to show us how he is feeling inside.

The painting is full of flowers . . . and animals. Can you spot the tiny creatures hiding in this scene?

ANSWERS

FRUIT AND FLOWERS IN A TERRACOTTA VASE, 1777–8
JAN VAN OS

All kinds of flowers and fruit are spilling out of this vase and tumbling onto the table. Jan van Os painted every tiny detail very carefully. From the droplets of water to the curling tulip petals – this picture looks so real we can almost smell the flowers!

A stunning painting needs a stunning frame.
Can you complete this one?

BACCHUS AND ARIADNE, 1520–3
TITIAN

Titian was a painter during the Renaissance – a golden time in the history of art. Renaissance painters chose big subjects for their work, such as epic Greek myths and legends. The artist has used colourful oil paints to bring his masterpiece to life.

This lady has some unusual pets.
Draw some more animal friends for her.

A LADY WITH A SQUIRREL AND A STARLING, about 1526–8
Hans Holbein the younger

Hamsters, dogs and kittens weren't such popular pets in England in the 1500s — instead people kept animals like squirrels, falcons and tiny monkeys! This lady is holding her squirrel on a little chain, while her starling perches on her shoulder.

This lady has been painted in profile.
Try to draw yourself this way.

PORTRAIT OF A LADY, about 1465
ALESSO BALDOVINETTI

A side view of a portrait is called a profile. This painting shows a lady wearing a very fine dress. The three leaves embroidered on her sleeve are palms. They were probably the emblem of the family that she was going to marry into.

Turner was a master at painting the setting sun.
Can you create your own beautiful sunset?

THE FIGHTING TEMERAIRE, 1839
Joseph Mallord William Turner

Joseph Turner is a much-loved English artist. He became known as 'the painter of light'. This picture shows a famous warship making its last voyage into a golden sunset.

Can you spot five differences between these two images?

ANSWERS

MARRIAGE A-LA MODE: I, THE MARRIAGE SETTLEMENT, about 1743
WILLIAM HOGARTH

This is the first in a collection of six paintings by William Hogarth that tells the story of a marriage between a wealthy couple. The artist liked to use his paintings to poke fun and comment on the rich people he saw around him. His paintings were full of tiny details that added to the main story he wanted to tell.

What a lovely day for messing about in the water!
Add some bathers about to jump in.

BATHERS AT LA GRENOUILLÈRE, 1869
CLAUDE MONET

The river in Claude Monet's scene looks irresistible —
gentle waves lap against the rowing boats and sunlight
dances on the water. The brushstrokes are broad and
simple, yet this painting perfectly captures this warm
day in Paris.

Fill this stall with fruit and veg! Use your pencil to add more cauliflowers, apples and pears . . .

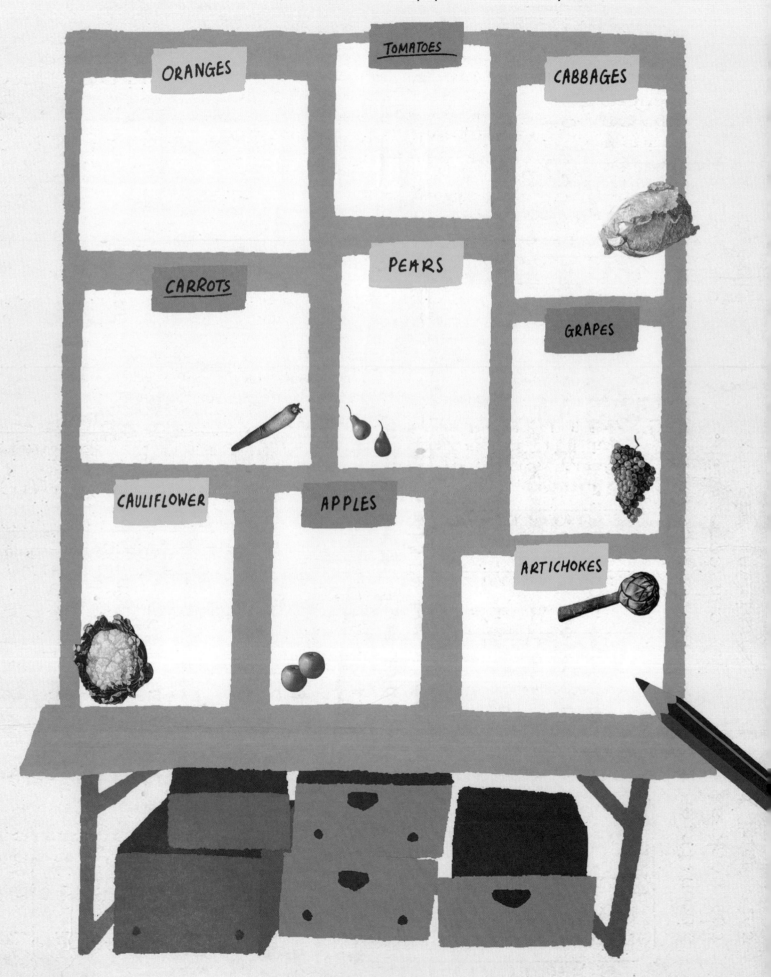

THE FOUR ELEMENTS: EARTH, 1569
JOACHIM BEUCKELAER

The cart in this painting by Joachim Beuckelaer is full with delicious market produce. Some of the colours have faded over the centuries. The sky would originally have been blue and the pink cabbages a deeper red!

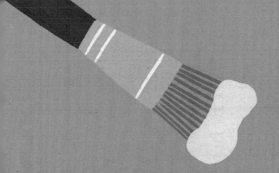

This painting is filled with warm red tones.
Can you create a picture using one single colour?

COMBING THE HAIR, about 1896
HILARIE-GERMAIN-EDGAR DEGAS

Ouch! This girl doesn't seem to be enjoying having her hair brushed. Degas cleverly covered his canvas with red colours to help us understand how she might be feeling. The oil paint shades are hot and uncomfortable.